FEELING SECURE IN A TROUBLED WORLD

BY

CHARLES F. STANLEY

THOMAS NELSON
Since 1798

NASHVILLE   DALLAS   MEXICO CITY   RIO DE JANEIRO

Published in Nashville, Tennessee, by Thomas Nelson, Inc.

Editing, layout, and design by Gregory C. Benoit Publishing, Old Mystic, CT

Unless otherwise noted, Scripture quotations are from The New King James Version. Copyright © 1979, 1980, 1982, Thomas Nelson Publishers.

Scripture quotations noted KJV are from the King James Version.

Scripture quotations noted NIV are from the Holy Bible:

ISBN 9781418543754

Printed in the United States of America

Contents

A Focus on Faith, Not Fear

God's Word commands us not to give in to fear and anxiety. Yet there can be times when this seems hard to do, when the uncertainties of life threaten us, or some grave calamity befalls us. Yet it is precisely at those times when the Lord's command is most pertinent: do *not* be afraid!

The Lord provides us all the resources we need to overcome fear, and our part is to trust Him in faith. In the following lessons, we will examine those resources, but at the outset you need to understand one fundamental principle: your faith is your best resource for overcoming fear and for bringing God's positive solutions to bear on negative circumstances.

In a study about security in troubled times, it is easy to get sidetracked into discussions about the latest negative news, the most recent wave of trouble, or the most recent crime statistics. It is also easy to stray into discussions about self-preservation, hoarding resources, or new means of self-protection. Avoid those tendencies! Stay focused on what the Bible has to say about your *faith*—making it strong, alive, active, and effective.

This book can be used by you alone or by several people in a small-group study. At various times, you will be asked to relate to the material in one of these four ways:

1. *What new insights have you gained?* Make notes about the insights that you have. You may want to record them in your Bible or in a separate

1

journal. As you reflect back over your insights, you are likely to see how God has moved in your life.

2. *Have you ever had a similar experience?* Each of us approaches the Bible from a unique background—our own particular set of relationships and experiences. Our experiences do not make the Bible true—the Word of God is truth regardless of our opinion about it. It is important, however, to share our experiences in order to see how God's truth can be applied to human lives.

3. *How do you feel about the material presented?* Emotional responses do not give validity to the Scriptures, nor should we trust our emotions as a gauge for our faith. In small-group Bible study, however, it is good for participants to express their emotions. The Holy Spirit often communicates with us through this unspoken language.

4. *In what way do you feel challenged to respond or to act?* God's Word may cause you to feel inspired or challenged to change something in your life. Take the challenge seriously and find ways of acting upon it. If God reveals to you a particular need that He wants *you* to address, take that as "marching orders" from God. God is expecting you to *do* something with the challenge that He has just given you.

Start and conclude your Bible study sessions in prayer. Ask God to give you spiritual eyes to see and spiritual ears to hear. As you conclude your study, ask the Lord to seal what you have learned so that you will never forget it. Ask Him to help you grow into the fullness of the stature of Christ Jesus.

Again, I caution you to keep the Bible at the center of your study. A genuine Bible study stays focused on God's Word and promotes a growing faith and a closer walk with the Holy Spirit in *each* person who participates.

LESSON 1

God's Provision in Times of Trouble

┌─────────────── ∾ **In This Lesson** ∾ ───────────────┐

LEARNING: How can I hope to find security in a world of danger and sorrow?

GROWING: What role does faith play in times of trial?

─────────────── ∾ ───────────────
└───┘

Everywhere we look in our world today, we see signs of very real trouble and danger. The troubles include natural disasters such as earthquakes, hurricanes, tornadoes, wildfires, and floods. They also include man-made dangers: chemical weapons, terrorist bombings, and conditions that lead to stock market meltdowns, rampant rioting, and coups intended to topple governments.

It seems at times that everything that *can* be shaken is being shaken in our world, from the shaking of the natural earth to the shaking of the world's financial systems, from the shaking of time-honored institutions and traditions to the shaking of personal values and morals. We seem to live in an unsteady and insecure world.

All of us walk through countless metal detectors and have our movements monitored by security cameras, perhaps far more than we are aware. Most people live behind double-locked doors, many live behind security gates or have their possessions protected by security systems, and some even arm themselves with personal weapons.

3

Countless people are too afraid of violent attack to take a walk in their own neighborhoods after dark.

For many, the terror is far more personal—fear that a spouse may come home drunk and become abusive, fear that a former spouse may turn to violent revenge, or fear of anger erupting from a total stranger in a public place. For some, the fear is rooted in suspicion, conjecture, and unconfirmed symptoms—fear of disease, fear that a child may be using drugs, or fear that a job may end tomorrow.

Is anything sure anymore? Can anything be counted on as being lasting, secure, and unchanging? How is a Christian supposed to live in an insecure world? Those questions are at the heart of this Bible study.

Triumphant Over Trials

There are three key biblical principles that I offer to you at the outset of this study. They are foundational principles that I hope you will remember as you study each lesson.

First, every person alive today faces sorrow, trouble, persecution, heartache, or a time of trial at some point in his life. Even if you are not experiencing trouble at this very moment, you very likely have experienced it in the fairly recent past, and with a great degree of certainty, I predict that you will experience trouble at some point in the future! None of us is immune to times of heartache, grief, trouble, and unsettling change. Trouble is a fact of life.

Loved ones die. Storms develop. Markets rise and fall. Relationships change, and the evil in many hearts continues to reign in prideful rebellion against God. We live in a fallen world.

Rather than see this as totally negative news, however, I encourage you to see a good side to this fact: you are not alone in your struggle with insecurity or trouble. Others have experienced what you are experiencing. No matter what type of trouble seems to be overwhelming you, there is another person—usually far closer than you think—who knows from firsthand experience what you are going through and how you feel.

Yet another piece of good news is this: men and women through the ages have experienced great persecutions, natural disasters, epidemics, wars, and trauma. Many of them were Christians, and they give us shining examples of how to respond to trials with faith by their overcoming lives, and by the words that they have used to document their experiences.

The book of 1 Peter was written to a group of people who were facing a coming tidal wave of persecution and hardship. Much of what we will cover in this Bible study is based upon 1 Peter. Peter's words are like a beacon of light in a frightening world—both then and now.

Ultimately, the good news is that Christ Jesus knows your struggle with fear, doubt, and insecure feelings. He became fully human so that He might experience all that you experience, and so that He might show us by example *how* to live triumphantly in difficult times.

Furthermore, Jesus Christ has sent the Holy Spirit to every person who believes in Him as Savior and who follows Him as Lord. The Holy Spirit is our great Comforter and Counselor in times of trial. He is present with us *always*, bringing to bear the awesome and unlimited power and presence of almighty God in any situation. You are *not* alone in your struggle. And you never will be alone in any struggle that you ever face!

Second, regardless of the type of trial or trouble that you experience, you have been given a wonderful gift from God to overcome it: faith. Faith is not a nebulous entity that floats in and out of our lives in unknown quantities or in a mysterious way. Faith is an *ability* that has been imparted to every human being. No person is without faith, even though you may feel at times that your faith has vanished or that it is at a very low ebb.

Faith is an awesome power. It is the power that motivates us to act with confidence and boldness. It is the power that activates the work of the Holy Spirit in us and through us. It is the power that brings about *change.* It is the force within us which enables us to endure hardship until God resolves the situation, turning it around so that His plans and purposes are enacted on earth. Through such faith, our purpose in life is fulfilled, rewards are given for our eternal benefit, and His glory is revealed.

Each of us has been given the power to overcome fear. We have been given the power to bring about *change* in our personal lives and in our world.

What trouble or difficulty are you currently experiencing? What role does faith play in your response to that trial?

6

↞ How does Christ's promise to protect you—spirit, mind, and body—influence your views of that trial?

Third, no trial or period of trouble lasts forever. At times, you may feel as if you have always experienced struggle or hardship. Some people seem to be hounded by troubles and trials all their lives. But the good news for every Christian is this: all problems, trials, and troubles end the instant we enter into eternity.

We also need to recognize that most troubles and trials do *not* last a lifetime. We often experience seasons of hardship or difficulty, instances of turmoil, and moments of crisis. These times of trouble may last a day, a month, a year—possibly even longer. But they do end.

If we maintain an active faith, trusting the Lord to work in us and to teach us and to strengthen us in our time of trial, we have the assurance that we will emerge from our troubling experience stronger in faith, wiser in His ways, more confident in His power, and more like Jesus. Trials and troubles are often used by the Lord to chisel us, sand us, and mold us into greater conformity to the likeness of Jesus' character.

A Rainbow After the Rain

God gave Noah a sign after the great flood: a rainbow appeared in the sky. With the rainbow, the Lord promised that He would never again completely destroy the earth by water. It was a promise that life would begin again, that the generations would continue, and that life had the potential for being better than it ever had been before.

The Lord holds out this same promise to each of us as we face troubled times. The Lord will walk with us *through* our trial all the way to the other side. His pledge to us is that our lives as Christians will *never end*. A new beginning is always possible for us—if not on earth, certainly in our heavenly home. The work that we have done for the Lord *will* last and reap eternal benefit. Our life in the future will be vastly superior to our life in the past, in the form of both earthly blessings and eternal rewards.

Be encouraged today. We *can* feel secure even in the midst of a world that is being shaken to its foundation.

My brethren, count it all joy when you fall into various trials, knowing that the testing of your faith produces patience. But let patience have its perfect work, that you may be perfect and complete, lacking nothing.

—James 1:2–4

Why does James tell us to "count it all joy" when trials come? What does this mean? How is it done?

What does it mean to "let patience have its perfect work"? How is this done? What role does faith play in these two steps?

❧ Today and Tomorrow ❧

TODAY: THE LORD HAS GIVEN ME THE GIFT OF FAITH, ENABLING ME TO STAND FIRM IN HARDSHIP.

TOMORROW: I WILL ASK THE LORD TO TEACH ME HOW TO INCREASE MY FAITH IN THE COMING WEEK.

❧ Notes and Prayer Requests: ❧

LESSON 2

The Foundation for Our Security

────────── ❧ **In This Lesson** ☙ ──────────

LEARNING: WHAT DOES BEING A CHRISTIAN HAVE TO DO WITH FACING
TRIALS?

GROWING: WHAT DOES GOD GIVE ME TO HELP ME THROUGH HARDSHIPS?

────────── ⬟ ──────────

In his first epistle, Peter was writing to a group of people who were anticipating a tidal wave of persecution and hardship under Roman Emperor Nero. A severe persecution of Christians in Rome had been instigated by Nero, and that wave of persecution was rapidly making its way eastward to the region of Asia Minor, which included Pontus, Galatia, Cappadocia, and Bithynia. Peter was writing to the churches that had been established in this region, whose members were bracing themselves against a time of trial. Nobody knew how severe or widespread the persecution might be, or how long it might last.

Peter, of course, knew about suffering and difficult times. He had watched Jesus be severely maligned, tortured, and crucified. He had witnessed the persecution of the early church by zealous Jews, first in Jerusalem and later in other cities throughout the area that we know as modern Israel. He had also been imprisoned on several occasions for the gospel's sake.

Peter's message is not one of dire warning or doom, however. His letter is filled with hope and the message of God's grace. His exhortation to the believers is that they must continue to stand firm in the faith. Peter writes to encourage the believers, and he gives them two main reasons why they can feel secure even though hard times are on the horizon. In this lesson, we will explore these reasons, which are the cornerstone of any believer's security.

You Have Been Chosen by God

From the opening lines of his letter, Peter makes a bold statement that the Christians to whom he is writing have been *chosen* by God:

> Grace and peace be multiplied to you in the knowledge of God and of Jesus our Lord, as His divine power has given to us all things that pertain to life and godliness, through the knowledge of Him who called us by glory and virtue, by which have been given to us exceedingly great and precious promises, that through these you may be partakers of the divine nature, having escaped the corruption that is in the world.

> —2 Pet. 1:2–4

What things "pertain to life and godliness"? List some examples below.

Life
godliness
great and precious Promises
may be partakers, having escaped
the Corruption

12

🐚 How do the things you listed in the previous question help you to combat fear and anxiety? How do those things increase your faith in God's character?

Stand firm in our faith
Grace & Peace

Peter makes it very clear that God has given the believers four wonderful things:

- 🐚 all things that pertain to life and godliness
- 🐚 a call to experience the Lord and to truly know Him
- 🐚 exceedingly great and precious promises that develop the nature of Christ
- 🐚 an escape from the corruption of the world

As believers today, we have been given these same great gifts from God.

Gift 1: All things pertaining to life and godliness. The good news is this: even though the world around us may be a boiling cauldron of sin, we do not need to partake of that sin. We can live free of it in our hearts and minds. Sinful human beings may hurt us, but they cannot force us to sin against God in our hearts. We can remain in right standing before the Father, regardless of what any other person may say or do.

Furthermore, as believers in Christ, we have the sure hope of eternal life. Indeed, we are already living in that hope—no matter what happens to us, we will never be separated from our loving heavenly Father. Even though the world around us may be filled with death, we can choose to pursue life. Even if we ourselves face death, we can know with certainty that we have the gift of eternal life.

> Jesus said to her, "I am the resurrection and the life. He who believes in Me, though he may die, he shall live. And whoever lives and believes in Me shall never die. Do you believe this?"
>
> —John 11:25, 26

↪ What did Jesus mean by "though he may die, he shall live"?

lives and believes in Me shall never die

↪ What is required to receive this gift from God? Have you taken that step?

Gift 2: A call to experience the Lord and to truly know Him. No matter how difficult the circumstances around us may become, as long as we are alive, we have the opportunity to grow in our knowledge of the Lord Jesus Christ, to grow in our relationship with our loving heavenly Father, and to grow in our capacity to experience God's love and mercy.

Peter wrote of the "sufferings of Christ and the glories that would follow" (1 Pet. 1:11). No matter what degree of pain and sorrow we may feel, Christ has felt that same pain and sorrow—and far more. Our ability to identify with Christ can grow through suffering if we will choose to see our suffering as an opportunity to know Him better.

When tragedies strike us, we can take one of two responses: to press in to God and know Him better and rely on Him more fully, or to blame God and withdraw from Him. In 1 Peter 1, Peter calls the believers in Asia Minor to choose to draw ever closer to God when persecution comes.

> Yet indeed I also count all things loss for the excellence of the knowledge of Christ Jesus my Lord, for whom I have suffered the loss of all things, and count them as rubbish, that I may gain Christ . . . that I may know Him and the power of His resurrection, and the fellowship of His sufferings, being conformed to His death.
>
> —Philippians 3:8, 10

What does it mean to be conformed to Jesus' death? How is this done? What role might hardship and suffering play in that process?

15

⬥ What does it mean to know "the fellowship of His sufferings"? What is required of us to be part of that fellowship?

dependanced provision & protection
we learn more to trust God.
he is utterly trustworthy. He never
fails us or forsakes us. He is present
with us always to comfort us.
guide us & help us.

Gift 3: Exceedingly great and precious promises that lead to our developing the character of Christ. What do we learn as we go through hard times and press on to know God better? We learn greater and greater dependence upon God. We ultimately learn that there is no one else on whom we can depend completely for the provision and protection that we need. All other systems, and eventually all other people—even those who love us—will fail us, because they are finite, limited human beings. The more we learn to trust God, the more we learn that He is utterly trustworthy. He never fails us or forsakes us. He is present with us always to comfort us, guide us, and help us.

Jesus said of Himself that He only did what He first saw the Father doing (John 5:19). He was under the authority of the Father. He drew every aspect of His life, being, character, and ability from the Father. His miracle-working and healing power was the Father's power. The mercy, love, and forgiveness that He extended were the mercy, love, and forgiveness of the Father.

Jesus lived in the Father's presence, filled with the Father's own nature, even in a world that rejected Him, ridiculed Him, and eventually killed Him. We are called to live in the same state of dependence upon the Father. No matter what anyone does to us, no matter what may happen to us, we are to draw our identity and our character from the Father. We are to respond to negative situations as Christ Jesus would respond. We are to live in the joy and peace of our relationship with the Lord, even when nothing around us seems joyous or at peace.

We are not called simply to *know* Christ, but to *learn* Christ—to become like Him and to manifest His character to the world around us.

☜ What are some of the "exceedingly great and precious promises" of Scripture? List some below.

☜ How can these promises strengthen your faith when you are facing trials?

Gift 4: A genuine escape from the corruption of the world. Peter and the other apostles knew that the real persecutor of our lives is not a storm, a condition, a disease, or another human being. The true persecutor of the believer is Satan. He is the one who seeks to steal, kill, and destroy. He is the one who seeks to ensnare us in sin to the point that we not only suffer in sin, but die in sin.

The true escape for the believers in Asia Minor was not an escape from Rome—it was the escape from Satan's snare which they had already experienced. Our true escape today is not from a negative situation but from the deadly nature of unforgiven sin.

Nothing can separate us from the love and mercy of God once we have accepted Jesus Christ as our Savior. We are eternally bound to Him. We are eternally secure in His forgiveness. We are no longer in our sins and trespasses—the life that we live is the eternal life of Christ Jesus.

> You are of God, little children, and have overcome [the evil spirits], because He who is in you is greater than he who is in the world.
>
> —1 John 4:4

🔊 According to this verse, how have you overcome the power of Satan?

We are no longer in our sins and trespasses, the life that we live is the eternal life of Christ Jesus. You are of God little children and are come evil spirits

If we confess our sins, He is faithful and just to forgive us our sins and to cleanse us from all unrighteousness. If we say that we have not sinned, we make Him a liar, and His word is not in us.

—1 John 1:9, 10

☙ According to these verses, what is our role in defeating Satan?

The God who has given me all things pertaining to life & godliness
God has promised me great promises
God who is conforming me the bondage of sin, and unto freed with me and me eternal life

Ask yourself today: Will the God who has given me all things pertaining to life and godliness; the God who has called me to experience Christ and to know Him; the God who has given me great promises; the God who is conforming me to the image of Christ Jesus; the God who has freed me from the bondage of sin and given me eternal life—will that God abandon me in a time of hardship? Never!

God has a purpose for your life. He has elected you, chosen you, selected you to live with Him forever. He is in the process of transforming you and conforming you into His own nature. He is perfecting you and making you whole—restoring you to the original design that He had in mind for you from eternity past. You are His child. Even in the most dire circumstances, you can live with a deep, inner assurance that God is with you and His Spirit resides within you.

Sealed by the Holy Spirit

Paul's second great message of hope and encouragement to the believers in Asia Minor was this: you are guarded and made safe by the power of God. The devil cannot penetrate the seal of the Holy Spirit on your life. The devil has no authority over your future. He cannot steal your divine inheritance or keep you from receiving God's promise of eternal life. Paul wrote to the Romans:

> Who shall separate us from the love of Christ? Shall tribulation, or distress, or persecution, or famine, or nakedness, or peril, or sword? . . . Yet in all these things we are more than conquerors through Him who loved us. For I am persuaded that neither death nor life, nor angels nor principalities nor powers, nor things present nor things to come, nor height nor depth, nor any other created thing, shall be able to separate us from the love of God which is in Christ Jesus our Lord.
>
> —Romans 8:35, 37–39

❧ According to these verses, what can separate you from the love of God? How does this relate to trials and hardships?

20

🖎 What does it mean to be "more than conquerors"? What more do we have in Christ besides victory over Satan?

The presence of God in the life of the believer is a certainty. God has called us and chosen us, He now indwells us, and He will never depart from us. The work that He has begun in us, He will finish. He will continue it until we are perfected and made whole according to His definition of perfection and wholeness. His presence with us abides forever.

In summary, the two great messages of Peter are:

🖎 God has chosen you as His beloved child and has given you the privilege of growing into the likeness of His Son, Jesus Christ, and of experiencing an intimate, eternal relationship with Him.

🖎 God is with you, now and forever, and He will keep all the promises that He has made to you in His Word.

Our security is based upon these two truths. God is with us—indeed, He dwells within us by the power of His Spirit—and He has a plan for us. These truths form the bedrock of our security. They are solid footing for us when all of the sands seem to be shifting around us.

In Him you also trusted, after you heard the word of truth, the gospel of your salvation; in whom also, having believed, you were sealed with the Holy Spirit of promise, who is the guarantee of our inheritance until the redemption of the purchased possession, to the praise of His glory.

—Ephesians 1:13, 14

What does it mean to be "sealed" with the Holy Spirit? What does this seal do? Who or what can remove it?

In what sense is the Holy Spirit the guarantee of your inheritance? What is that inheritance? What role does the Holy Spirit play in the process of your redemption?

Today and Tomorrow

TODAY: I HAVE BEEN CHOSEN BY GOD AND SEALED WITH HIS SPIRIT—FOR ALL ETERNITY!

TOMORROW: I WILL SPEND TIME IN GOD'S WORD EACH DAY IN ORDER TO LEARN MORE OF CHRIST.

Notes and Prayer Requests:

A Proper Perspective in a Time of Trouble

❧ In This Lesson ☙

LEARNING: WHAT AM I SUPPOSED TO LEARN FROM MY PRESENT TRIAL?

GROWING: HOW DOES GOD WANT ME TO REACT IN THIS SITUATION?

How are we to respond to troubled times? How are we to respond to distressing circumstances or an inner heaviness that doesn't seem to lift? First and foremost, we are to adopt a right perspective of our problem. In 1 Peter, we find five things to do when we face times of struggle, hardship, persecution, or pain. Each of these actions is related to our developing and maintaining a godly perspective.

Key 1: Reaffirm Our Position in Christ

As we studied in the last lesson, Peter established a foundation for the believers in Asia Minor who were facing impending persecution. He encouraged them that their security should always be based upon the fact that they were chosen in Christ forever, and that they were always guarded and guided by an omnipotent God.

The foremost thing you can do when facing trouble is to *reaffirm your position in Christ*. Make your position in Christ the perspective from which you view trouble. As you face a time of trial, choose to see yourself as being saved, loved, and in relationship with an all-powerful, ever-present heavenly Father. As a believer, you are also part of the body of Christ—you are not alone.

Abigail stated her case before King David: "The life of my lord shall be bound in the bundle of the living with the LORD your God; and the lives of your enemies He shall sling out, as from the pocket of a sling" (1 Sam. 25:29). This is the same position in which we find ourselves—we are "bound to the bundle" of those whose souls have been redeemed by the Lord.

⟊ What does it mean to be "bound in the bundle of the living"? Why is it significant that this condition is "with the LORD your God"?

⟊ A sling was a weapon of warfare, used by David to slay Goliath. Why does Abigail use that metaphor? What does this teach about how God will resolve your trials?

25

There are several facts that we must believe and reaffirm as we see ourselves in Christ:

1. No problem has the power to tear us from the grasp of Christ.
2. No difficulty can do more harm than Christ can remedy.
3. No trial can destroy our salvation.
4. No pain or heartache is too great for Christ to heal.

Key 2: Reaffirm That Your Trial Will Be Profitable

There is a vast difference between the person who views a trial as an irresolvable, devastating calamity and the person who views a trial as a difficulty from which he might learn and grow. The person who sees a trial as one-hundred percent negative is going to benefit little from that trial and is going to feel dejected, fearful, and frustrated for its duration. In contrast, the person who sees a trial as having at least some benefit is going to be looking for that benefit—and finding it. He is going to feel more optimistic and hopeful and is likely to work harder to overcome the trial.

There are three questions that we should ask in a time of trial:

1. What is the source of this trial? Some troubles are brought about by our own ignorance, negligence, or willful rebellion. If trouble comes into our lives in one of these ways, the way out of the trouble is likely to be the opposite of what got us into trouble! We may need more wisdom or information, we may need to be more diligent or careful, or we may need to repent of our rebellion and obey God's commandments.

If the trial or trouble is a natural disaster, we may need to reevaluate what we can do to prevent such a disaster in the future. None of us can make our lives completely catastrophe-proof, but we can be wise about where we build, how we live, and what materials we use in our homes. We can build shelters from storms, and we can heed evacuation warnings. If the trial or trouble is in a relationship, improving the relationship may be a solution, perhaps through mutual counseling.

Take a close look at the source of the trial. You'll likely find ways in which you can turn things around so that you regain what you have lost, and you also might improve your situation and prevent future trials.

&. When have you faced a trial that was brought about by external circumstances? What did you learn from that experience? How have you avoided repeating it?

&. When have you faced a trial that was brought about by your own action or inaction? What did you learn from that experience? How have you avoided repeating it?

2. What is the reason that God has allowed this trial in my life? God has allowed you to experience this struggle for a sovereign purpose. There is very likely something that He desires to build, grow, change, or heal in your life, or in the life of someone close to you. Ask God to reveal His purpose.

Too many people blame God for their problems—but God does not punish His children by sending them problems. Others believe that all problems are from the enemy of their souls. They fail to recognize that God knew about the problem long before it arose and could have averted it if He had so desired. God may not create or instigate problems in our lives, but He does *allow* them. He uses problems to teach us valuable lessons. He allows problems so that we might change our ways and become stronger, wiser, and more whole.

When has God used a trial in your life to teach you or strengthen you? What did you gain from it?

What is your natural response when troubles arise? Do you tend to blame God, blame others, or blame yourself? Or do you instinctively look for God's blessings?

3. What is the potential result of this situation? Look for the best possible outcome. What might you learn? How might you grow through the experience? What benefits are possible? Romans 8:28 tells us, "We know that all things work together for good to those who love God, to those who are the called according to His purpose."

Peter was quick to see a good reason for the trials that were coming to the believers:

> In this you greatly rejoice, though now for a little while, if need be, you have been grieved by various trials, that the genuineness of your faith, being much more precious than gold that perishes, though it is tested by fire, may be found to praise, honor, and glory at the revelation of Jesus Christ, whom having not seen you love.

> —1 Peter 1:6–8

Peter regarded a trial as a time of testing, which he also likened to the refining process associated with fine metals. Gold and silver are put into blazing furnaces in order to liquefy them so that the dross, or the alloy metals, might rise to the top and be skimmed away, leaving the pure gold or silver behind. A trial can produce this same work in our lives. It can refine us and purify us so that we might bring greater praise, honor, and glory to Jesus Christ.

Why is genuine faith more precious than refined gold? How is such faith acquired?

❧ What is the outcome of trials and testing, according to these verses? Why does your genuine faith lead to God's glory rather than your own?

Key 3: See the Trial Against Eternity's Backdrop

A major shift occurs in our perspective when we take our eyes off our problem and put the focus on eternity. Against the backdrop of eternity, any trial that we might experience on earth is only momentary. When we get our eyes onto the wonderful future that we have with the Lord in heaven, any trouble or trial that we experience here is going to seem like a "light affliction" (2 Cor. 4:17). What is a little trouble here in the light of an eternal future of glory and splendor with the Lord?

> Therefore we do not lose heart. Even though our outward man is perishing, yet the inward man is being renewed day by day. For our light affliction, which is but for a moment, is working for us a far more exceeding and eternal weight of glory, while we do not look at the things which are seen, but at the things which are not seen. For the things which are seen are temporary, but the things which are not seen are eternal.
>
> —2 Corinthians 4:16–18

☙ What is "the inward man"? How is this separate from the "outward man"? How can one be dying while the other is being renewed?

☙ When have you experienced a trial that did not seem to last "for a moment"? How can comparing that with eternity change your opinion?

Key 4: Look for Ways That Your Faith Will Increase

As you face trials or troubles, focus on the ways in which your faith is going to work and grow.

First, anticipate that your faith will work. God has given you faith to use. He expects it to be effective in bringing about positive changes in your life, and in the lives of others around you.

Second, anticipate that your faith will become stronger as a result of the trouble you are experiencing. The more we use our faith, the stronger it becomes.

Third, anticipate that your faith will grow. The Bible describes three levels of faith:

ᐁ little faith—those who believe that God can help and hope that He will

ᐁ great faith—those who believe that God can help and that God will help

ᐁ perfect faith—those who believe that something is desired by God and, therefore, it is as good as done!

The Lord taught a parable in which He showed that our faith is proven and it grows and increases as we obey what the Lord tells us to do (Luke 17:5–10). Great faith does not blossom overnight. It is the result of years of trusting and obeying the Lord—including trusting and obeying the Lord during difficult times, in the presence of difficult people, and at difficult tasks.

And which of you, having a servant plowing or tending sheep, will say to him when he has come in from the field, "Come at once and sit down to eat"? But will he not rather say to him, "Prepare something for my supper, and gird yourself and serve me till I have eaten and drunk, and afterward you will eat and drink"? Does he thank that servant because he did the things that were commanded him? I think not.

—Luke 17:7–9

What principle is the Lord teaching in these verses? How does this principle apply to your faith? To your present trials?

Key 5: Look for Growth in Your Relationship

with Christ

Just as you look for your faith to strengthen and to grow, look for your relationship with Christ to deepen and become more precious. Every trial or time of trouble is an opportunity for you to trust Him more, love Him more, and find greater joy and contentment in your relationship with Him. As it has been said, "God uses 'where we are' to teach us 'who He is.'"

The more we see Christ Jesus in the midst of our trials, the more we find reason for genuine praise. We do not praise God *for* our situation, but *in* our situation. We do not praise God for the pain we feel, but for who He is as our Healer, Protector, Provider, Counselor, Comforter, and Friend. No matter how dark the day, it will seem brighter as we say, "Praise be to God! He is worthy to be praised!"

> Rejoice always, pray without ceasing, in everything give thanks; for this is the will of God in Christ Jesus for you.
>
> —1 Thessalonians 5:16–18

ও. What does it mean to give thanks in everything? How is this done? How is it different from giving thanks *for* everything?

ও. How does a person "pray without ceasing"? Why is this part of God's will for you?

Start with Your Perspective

Consider the two perspectives compared below:

Perspective 1	Perspective 2
confusion about whether one has a relationship with God	certain that one is bound together in Christ and is part of Christ's Body forever
doubtful that anything good can come from the present difficulty	optimistic that God can bring something good from the present trouble or difficulty
blames God and others for the problem and has no hope for the problem to be resolved unless others or circumstances change	looks for the source, reason, and result of the problem so that the problem can be addressed and resolved quickly
sees problem as monumental and lasting forever	sees problem as momentary in the light of eternity
regards a problem as contrary to faith or damaging to one's faith	regards a problem as having the potential to strengthen and increase one's faith

Before you can ever truly feel secure in a time of trouble, you must have the right perspective.

◈ Which of the perspectives in the preceding list do you tend to fall into? Which specific items in each perspective need to be addressed this week?

◈ Today and Tomorrow ◈

TODAY: GOD HAS AN ETERNAL PERSPECTIVE, AND HE USES TRIALS FOR MY ETERNAL BENEFIT.

TOMORROW: I WILL ASK THE LORD TO HELP ME THIS WEEK TO GAIN HIS PERSPECTIVE ON MY LIFE.

LESSON 4

The Unshakable Security of Our Salvation

❧ In This Lesson ❧

LEARNING: DOES THIS TRIAL MEAN THAT GOD IS ANGRY WITH ME, OR THAT I'M NOT A CHRISTIAN?

GROWING: HOW CAN I KNOW THAT I'M STILL SAVED WHEN HARDSHIPS COME?

Many Christians believe that when tough times come their way, God is angry with them. They fear that if God becomes angry enough or is angry often enough, He may withdraw their salvation. Part of their insecurity is related to their relationship with the Lord.

Do you ever wonder if you are experiencing a difficult trial because you have lost your salvation? Do you ever fear that you might be in danger of losing your salvation because of a crisis or time of trauma? If so, this lesson is especially for you!

What Does It Mean to Be Saved?

Confusion about one's salvation often results from a lack of understanding about what it really means to be saved. God does not save us because we have:

~ stopped bad behavior in order to "get right with God"

~ joined a church

~ knelt at an altar to say that we're sorry for our sins

~ added Christian disciplines such as prayer and Bible reading to our daily routines

All of these things are works of some kind, but salvation comes from faith. It is the result of believing, not a by-product of doing. Nicodemus, a very religious man in the time of Jesus, was shocked when Jesus told him that his good works as a law-keeping Jew were inadequate for him to be born again. Jesus said to him:

> Most assuredly, I say to you, unless one is born of water and the Spirit, he cannot enter the kingdom of God. That which is born of the flesh is flesh, and that which is born of the Spirit is spirit. Do not marvel that I said to you, "You must be born again." The wind blows where it wishes, and you hear the sound of it, but cannot tell where it comes from and where it goes. So is everyone who is born of the Spirit. . . .

> And as Moses lifted up the serpent in the wilderness, even so must the Son of Man be lifted up, that whoever believes in Him should not perish but have eternal life. For God so loved the world that He gave His only begotten Son, that whoever believes in Him should not perish but have everlasting life. For God did not send His Son into the world to condemn the world, but that the world through Him might be saved.

> He who believes in Him is not condemned; but he who does not believe is condemned already, because he has not believed in the name of the only begotten Son of God.

> —John 3:5–8, 14–18

~ What does it mean, in your own words, to be "born again"? Have you been born again?

~ Once a person is born, he can never again become "unborn." What does this suggest about being born again?

An Act of Believing and Receiving

Jesus told Nicodemus that the act of receiving God's provision for man's sin was a simple matter of believing. He referred to an Old Testament story in which the Israelites were experiencing a plague of poisonous snakes in their camp. All the Lord required of them was that they look upon the form of a bronze serpent lifted up on a pole, and they would live (see Num. 21:5–9).

Jesus said that this same pattern would hold true for those who "looked" upon His death on the Cross. All that a person needs to do today to be saved from the consequences of sin is to look at Jesus on the Cross, believing that Jesus was and is forever God's sole provision for man's sin. A belief in Jesus as God's Son and as God's sacrifice for the sins of man is what saves a person. *Nothing less will do, but nothing more is required.*

A Free Gift to All Who Receive It

Salvation is a free gift of God to those who will receive it. Salvation is not bestowed upon all mankind, however, whether wanted or not. We must *choose* by an act of faith to believe in Jesus and to receive Him as our Savior.

If you confess with your mouth the Lord Jesus and believe in your heart that God has raised Him from the dead, you will be saved. For with the heart one believes unto righteousness, and with the mouth confession is made unto salvation.

—Romans 10:9, 10

∽ Why does Paul insist that both the heart and the mouth are involved in accepting God's gift of salvation? What happens if one or the other is not involved?

∽ Do you believe that God raised Jesus from the dead? If not, what prevents you from believing? If so, tell someone else.

What Are We Saved From?

When we accept Jesus Christ as our Savior, we are not saved from difficulty, trial, or hardship in life. We are not saved from being tempted or from ever having an encounter with an evil person. When we receive Jesus Christ as our Savior, we are saved from the eternal consequences that are associated with a person's *sin nature*. Salvation is a matter of the heart of man—it is not a matter of outer circumstances or external situations.

Every Person Has a Choice to Make

The Bible makes it very clear that there are those who are saved and destined for eternal life with God, and those who are not saved and are destined for a life apart from God. Jesus spoke very clearly about this in Matthew 25:

> ✎ "Cast the unprofitable servant into the outer darkness. There will be weeping and gnashing of teeth" (v. 30).
> ✎ "He will also say to those on the left hand, 'Depart from Me, you cursed, into the everlasting fire prepared for the devil and his angels'" (v. 41).
> ✎ "These will go away into everlasting punishment, but the righteous into eternal life" (v. 46).

Those who choose to believe in Christ Jesus are saved. Each person must do his own believing. Nobody else can believe on our behalf.

Sin Is Man's Original Nature

Sin against God is going beyond the boundaries established by God. It is not only a behavioral problem, however—one rooted in attitudes, motives, actions, and patterns of conduct. Sin is a nature problem, an identity or state-of-being problem. Man's sin nature is one of pride, greed, and total self-centeredness and self-will. Every person is born with this sin nature. Behavior is learned; our natural tendency to sin is not. A sin nature is inherent, and it is inherent regardless of the spiritual condition of our parents. It is part of our inheritance as fallen human beings, the descendants of Adam.

Now, a person might change his or her behavior by an act of the will. But a person cannot change his basic sin nature, no matter how much willpower is exerted. We are incapable of transforming our spirits or of altering the core of our spiritual being. We are born with a sin condition that only God can correct.

The good news is that, while we were in this helpless state of unforgiven sin, God sent His Son Jesus to die for us so that we do not have to experience the consequence of our sin nature, which is separation and alienation from God. We can be transformed and made new in spirit through believing in Him.

> But God demonstrates His own love toward us, in that while we were still sinners, Christ died for us.

> —Romans 5:8

☙ Why did Jesus die? Why did His death pay the penalty for your sins?

43

❧ Why was God willing to have His Son pay your debt? Why was Jesus willing to die?

What Happens When We Accept Christ?

Two things happen simultaneously to a person who believes in and receives Jesus as his Savior:

1. Those who believe in Jesus and accept Him as their Savior receive an everlasting quantity of life. Jesus said to Nicodemus, "Whoever believes . . . should not perish but have everlasting life" (John 3:16). In many versions of the Bible, the word *should* is translated "will" or "shall." Whoever believes will undeniably be given everlasting life by God. Jesus also said:

> Let not your heart be troubled; you believe in God, believe also in Me. In My Father's house are many mansions; if it were not so, I would have told you. I go to prepare a place for you. And if I go and prepare a place for you, I will come again and receive you to Myself; that where I am, there you may be also. And where I go you know, and the way you know.
>
> —John 14:1–4

🖎 Why does Jesus say, "You believe in God, believe also in Me"? Why is a belief in God necessary before one can believe in Jesus?

🖎 What did Jesus mean when He said, "Where I go you know, and the way you know"? What is He speaking of? What is "the way"?

2. Those who believe in Jesus and accept Him as their Savior receive a new quality of life. Jesus also said to Nicodemus, "That which is born of the Spirit is spirit" (John 3:6). The Holy Spirit is sent to you by Jesus Christ the very instant you believe in Christ. It is the Spirit who causes your spirit to be reborn or made new. There are two very important things that you need to know about this rebirth by the Spirit:

The Spirit does the birthing. You cannot will it to be done. Your part is to believe and receive. When we believe, the Holy Spirit enters into us and causes our old sin nature to be transformed into a new nature that is in the likeness of God. The transformation of our spirit is a sovereign work of God.

Part of believing is confessing your sins, which means to acknowledge your sins. Confessing is owning up to your own sin nature and saying to the Lord, "I am a sinner. I have a sin nature. I ask You to forgive my sin nature and give me a new nature, with a heart to serve You. I believe in Jesus as the Savior and I receive Him into my life." When we receive Christ, God immediately acts to transform our spiritual nature.

Once a person has received the Holy Spirit into his life, he will have a desire to love God, serve God, and walk in the ways of God. The person who is truly born anew spiritually will *want* to live according to God's commandments and to follow the daily leading of the Holy Spirit. The gift of the Holy Spirit is to help us walk in this new way of life.

We often hear the word *repentance* in association with salvation. To repent is to have a change of mind. The Holy Spirit will cause a person to *want* to have a change of mind and, therefore, a subsequent change of behavior. Repentance comes in the wake of our salvation; it is the outgrowth of our receiving Christ.

Repentance and change come not only as the Holy Spirit prompts us, but also as the Holy Spirit helps us to make changes! The Holy Spirit is our enabler—He functions within us as the Spirit of Truth and the giver of courage and power. It is His power that links to our will to give us the only source of genuine *willpower* that we can ever really have.

Nothing can alter God's definitive work in us. It is vitally important for you to understand that you cannot save yourself—and it is equally important for you to understand that you cannot unsave yourself. Once a baby is born and is delivered from his mother's body, he can never go back into the womb. The same is true for us spiritually.

Once the Holy Spirit has birthed us into the family of God, delivering us from sin's bondage and giving us a brand-new nature, nothing that we do can ever cause the Spirit to unbirth us. The same holds true for any other influence, person, circumstance, or time of trouble. *Nothing* can affect our salvation once we are born anew spiritually. Our salvation is a certainty with God.

Furthermore, nothing can keep the Holy Spirit from continuing His transforming work in our lives. The Holy Spirit will continue to work within us until the moment we die. Now we may reject His work. We may turn our backs on His convicting voice in our spirit. We may ignore His warnings. We may choose to go our own way. But we cannot separate ourselves from His efforts to mold us and conform us to the character and likeness of Christ Jesus.

Therefore, if anyone is in Christ, he is a new creation; old things have passed away; behold, all things have become new.

—2 Corinthians 5:17

47

 What "old things" passed away when you accepted Christ as your Savior? What things became new?

my life change for the good. New thing's were much for health, the Lord has built me of many things in my life,

 If those old things "passed away" (i.e., died), what does that suggest about the security of your salvation?

 What is the work of the Holy Spirit in making all things new? What is your role in that process?

The Holy Spirit's Convicting Presence

Prior to our salvation, the Holy Spirit presents Christ to us and convicts us of our need to receive Him. We can turn a deaf ear to His message so that we no longer hear it. That does not mean, however, that the Spirit ceases to speak. We simply have become so hardened in our unbelief that we refuse to hear.

After we are saved, the Holy Spirit convicts us to repent and make changes in our lives so that we might experience greater wholeness and greater blessings from God. We can turn a deaf ear to His message, but He never quits speaking to us. The result will be that we are miserable and frustrated. The result will also be that we may enter into eternity without many rewards awaiting us. But we are not unsaved, nor have we lost our salvation.

When we feel conviction in our spirits, that is the work of the Holy Spirit calling us to greater conformity to Christ. It is not a conviction that we are unsaved.

> So then, those who are in the flesh cannot please God. But you are not in the flesh but in the Spirit, if indeed the Spirit of God dwells in you. Now if anyone does not have the Spirit of Christ, he is not His.
>
> —Romans 8:8, 9

What does it mean to be "in the flesh"? What does it mean to be "in the Spirit"?

⌐☙ Why does Paul say that anyone who does not have the Sprit is not one of God's children? Why are the two inseparable?

Your Salvation and Times of Trial

Here is the point at which many Christians err: they know that their faith is linked to their salvation. When a time of trial hits them, they find their faith shaken. They experience moments of doubt and fear, and they wrongly conclude that their lack of faith is related to a loss of salvation.

That is *not* what the Bible teaches. Your faith brought the Holy Spirit into your life. Your believing in Jesus allowed the Holy Spirit to transform your sin nature into a new nature. But your faith did not cause you to be saved. The saving work in you was done exclusively by the Holy Spirit.

The faith of the believer is infused with the faith of the Holy Spirit so that the believer can overcome evil, live a righteous life before God, understand God's Word as never before, and bring healing and deliverance to others in the name of Jesus Christ. A lack of faith can limit the effectiveness of a believer, but it cannot cause the Holy Spirit to leave that person's spirit.

When a time of trial hits, the proper response for the born-again believer in Christ Jesus is this:

> ~ God knows all about the situation and He knows all about me personally. He knows fully how this situation affects me, and He knows what He has planned and purposed in my life.
>
> ~ God loves me, has forgiven me from my sins, and by the power of His Holy Spirit, dwells within me. He is at work in me to perfect me, make me whole, and conform me to the character and likeness of Christ Jesus. He will not give up on His work in me.
>
> ~ No matter what happens to me, I can be completely secure in my spirit, knowing that I am in Christ and Christ is in me. I have an eternal home and a lasting, eternal, unshakable relationship with almighty God—my loving heavenly Father.
>
> ~ Nothing about the trial, grief, or pain that I am currently experiencing can change the fact of my salvation in any way.

Feeling secure in spirit is the best feeling of security that a person can ever have—and especially so when nothing else in a person's life seems certain. (If you would like to explore the topic of eternal security further, I encourage you to get the book in this study series entitled *Understanding Eternal Security*.)

I have been crucified with Christ; it is no longer I who live, but Christ lives in me; and the life which I now live in the flesh I live by faith in the Son of God, who loved me and gave Himself for me.

—Galatians 2:20

If you have been crucified, what power can anything now have over you? What can remove Christ, who now lives in you?

Why is faith so vital to living the new life of the born-again believer? What role does that faith play in obedience? In dealing with trials?

❧ Today and Tomorrow ❧

TODAY: NOTHING CAN EVER REMOVE ME FROM GOD'S FAMILY—NOTHING.

TOMORROW: WHEN TROUBLES ARISE THIS WEEK, I WILL RESPOND TO THEM IN THE SECURITY OF GOD'S LOVE.

❧ Notes and Prayer Requests: ❧

A Readiness for Rough Times

✎ In This Lesson ✎

LEARNING: WHY WOULD GOD LET ME GET HIT WITH THIS TRIAL WITHOUT ANY WARNING?

GROWING: HOW CAN I PREPARE IN ADVANCE FOR COMING HARDSHIP?

In many instances, rough times blindside us, seeming to come out of the blue. In other cases, however, we know that, in all likelihood, a tough time is inevitable. For example, parents might anticipate an empty nest as their teenagers mature and prepare to leave home; a family might anticipate grief as an elderly parent ages; a family might anticipate the rough time of moving and adjusting to a new city.

There is much that we can do to prepare for rough times, both in the natural and in the emotional realms of life. In this lesson, we will focus on five ways that Peter tells us to prepare ourselves spiritually for a potential time of trouble or persecution.

1. Gird Your Minds for Godly Action

In Bible times, both men and women wore long outer garments. These could become a hindrance to a person who might be running or walking swiftly, walking through streams, or working at certain tasks. At times, a person found it better to gird up a garment by tucking a portion of it into the girdle at the waist. To *gird up* literally means to secure with a girdle or a wide belt.

What does this mean to us in the spiritual realm? It means that we are to remove from our lives those things that are a hindrance to us. We are to have the right attitude, removing anger, fear, worry, resentment, or any other negative feeling that can keep us from focusing positively on getting through the rough time and emerging stronger and more whole in its aftermath. Peter writes:

> Therefore gird up the loins of your mind, be sober, and rest your hope fully upon the grace that is to be brought to you at the revelation of Jesus Christ; as obedient children, not conforming yourselves to the former lusts, as in your ignorance; but as He who called you is holy, you also be holy in all your conduct.

> —1 Peter 1:13–15

A person who enters a rough time focused on himself, simply living from day to day and following the whim of the moment, is going to feel doubly hit when a difficult time emerges. He will be unprepared emotionally for both the possibility and the reality of such a trial.

Peter called the believers to get serious about their lives and their future, to conform themselves to the holy character of Jesus Christ, and to remain hopeful. These are all attitudes that the believer must *choose* to adopt.

☜ What does it mean to "gird up the loins of your mind"? How is this done? Why is the mind an important element in facing trials? In living a holy life?

☜ What does it mean to "conform yourself" to lust? What role does deliberate choice play in that conformity? How does such conformity affect one's entire person?

2. Keep Sober in Your Spirit

Being sober in spirit does not mean that Christians should be long-faced, sorrowful creatures without any expression of joy or happiness! In fact, Jesus spoke very clearly that Christians *at no time* should reflect a lack of joy or hope in order to appear more pious (see Matt. 6:16–18). Even in troubled times, we are to remain hopeful and confident in our faith. To be sober means to:

- have balanced judgment
- exhibit a lack of panic
- be steady and watchful
- remain balanced

The sober person does not grab on to a quick-fix promise or heresy, but remains measured and deliberate in his believing and behaving. The sober person *responds* to life, rather than reacting to it.

Teaching us that, denying ungodliness and worldly lusts, we should live soberly, righteously, and godly in the present age, looking for the blessed hope and glorious appearing of our great God and Savior Jesus Christ, who gave Himself for us, that He might redeem us from every lawless deed and purify for Himself His own special people, zealous for good works.

—Titus 2:12–14

- What does it mean to live soberly? Give practical examples.

- What does it mean to be zealous for good works? Give practical examples.

3. Fix Your Hope on God's Grace

Peter wrote, "Rest your hope fully upon the grace that is to be brought to you at the revelation of Jesus Christ" (1 Pet. 1:13). To rest your hope fully means to set your hope, to fix it, to attach it firmly. Hope does not exist in a vacuum. It is always directed toward something that still lies ahead. It is aimed at something. Hope is not wishful thinking, as in, "I hope that tomorrow will be sunny." Hope is a confident assurance that something in the future will come to pass, an assurance that is based upon God's Word rather than on our own desires.

Peter tells the new believers to fix their hope firmly and fully on God's grace, on the loving work of God in our lives that is going to be revealed to them in the troubled time ahead. The Lord allows us to experience rough times so that He might accomplish His purposes in us, and then, through us, accomplish His purposes in the lives of others. Our hope, therefore, lies in the absolute certainty that the Lord's purposes will be fulfilled in us and in others.

As we prepare for a rough time, our spiritual attitude should be, "I know with certainty that God is going to bring me through this so that I become stronger, wiser, and more faithful in my walk with Him."

Now may the God of hope fill you with all joy and peace in believing, that you may abound in hope by the power of the Holy Spirit.

—Romans 15:13

∽ How does the hope that Paul is speaking of differ from the way most people use the word (as in, "I hope I get the job")? How is it different from wishful thinking?

∽ What hopes does the Bible provide to those who believe in Christ? How do such hopes provide joy and peace?

4. Do Not Fall Back into Your Old Life

There are times when a Christian faces a rough time, and, in panic, he reverts to old ways, habits, and patterns of thinking and responding. At other times, we see tough times ahead and we resort to the world's systems—we look to the way the world solves problems and avoids crises as a pattern for handling our own difficulties. Peter admonished the believers to avoid "conforming yourselves to the former lusts," which was the way, he said, they had lived in their ignorance before accepting Christ.

As believers, we have been given a new way of thinking and responding to life's problems. The old ways of thinking and responding that are habitual to us must be *put off*. We must choose to think and act in different ways. As you prepare yourself for a rough time, ask the Lord:

≈ How do You want me to face this problem and resolve it?

≈ How do You want me to prepare for this season that appears to be a difficult one?

≈ How do You want me to respond emotionally to this impending situation?

≈ What should I say or do in the coming situation that will be pleasing to You?

Too often, a person tries to escape the brunt of rough times by surrounding himself with a layer of material possessions. He hopes that a padding of luxury or material sufficiency will make the tough time easier to endure. Others turn to various substances and experiences that they hope will numb them to the coming pain or to the reality that they fear will be unpleasant.

The Lord desires that we face our rough times with boldness and confidence, trusting Him—and Him alone—to give us the comfort and the courage we need. The Lord desires that we face rough times with all of our faculties fully functioning. We need to stay physically and emotionally well and strong so that we can effectively face the coming crisis.

That you put off, concerning your former conduct, the old man which grows corrupt according to the deceitful lusts, and be renewed in the spirit of your mind, and that you put on the new man which was created according to God, in true righteousness and holiness.

—Ephesians 4:22–24

꼭 What does it mean to put off the old man? To put on the new man? How is each done? Why must the old be put off before the new can be put on?

꼭 What does it mean to "be renewed in the spirit of your mind"? How is this done, in practical terms?

5. Be Holy

Holiness is not an external demeanor, and it definitely is not a holier-than-thou attitude or a pious set of behaviors intended to impress another person. The Greek word translated as *holy* means "to be sanctified" or "to be cleansed and set apart" for God's purposes. As a Christian, you do not belong to yourself. You now belong to God—you are His child, His servant, His beloved witness. You have a separate identity from that of the world at large; you have become part of the family of God; you are no longer just a general member of the family of mankind.

To be holy means that we remain submissive to the Holy Spirit so that His holiness flows through us. Our righteousness is not something that we can manufacture, think up, or develop on our own. Our righteousness is *His* righteousness manifested in us.

In facing tough times, it is vitally important that you set your heart and mind to respond to the situations that you encounter *as Jesus Christ would respond.* Choose to see yourself as being part of the body of Christ, a beloved child of almighty God, your heavenly Father. Choose to respond in a godly way, in spite of what others may do to you or say about you. Choose to pursue a path of righteousness—which is saying and doing the right things from God's perspective—regardless of how you may feel in any given moment or situation. We must choose to be holy, and to allow the holiness of the Spirit to operate in our lives. Peter wrote, "As He who called you is holy, you also be holy in all your conduct, because it is written, 'Be holy, for I am holy'" (1 Pet. 1:15–16).

> Do not love the world or the things in the world. If anyone loves the world, the love of the Father is not in him. For all that is in the world—the lust of the flesh, the lust of the eyes, and the pride of life—is not of the Father but is of the world. And the world is passing away, and the lust of it; but he who does the will of God abides forever.
>
> —1 John 2:15–17

☙ Why is a love for the world completely incompatible with a love for God? Why can't a person love both?

☙ Define the following, giving examples of each:

Lust of the Flesh:

Lust of the Eyes:

Pride of Life:

Ready for Trouble

As you have read and studied the five ways in which Peter exhorted the early believers to be ready for a coming wave of persecution, you may have thought to yourself, "This is the way I should live *all* the time!" That's absolutely correct. If we choose to do the things that Peter said, we will live in a state of spiritual readiness for any problems that may come our way, expected or unexpected.

Gird your minds—remove from your life all attitudes that might hinder a rapid and effective response to trouble.

Keep sober in your spirit—watchful, balanced, and steady in your faith.

Fix your hope on the grace of God—which is, and will continue to be, manifested toward you.

Refuse to revert to old patterns, habits, and worldly ways of thinking and responding—choose to respond in a godly manner.

Invite the Holy Spirit to work in and through you so that you might express the true nature of God, your heavenly Father, to others around you.

The person who lives in this manner is ready for rough times—ready for *all* times and seasons of life!

↝ Grade your present performance in the following areas, where 1 = *nonexistent*, 3 = *average*, and 5 = *stellar*.

Gird your mind: 1   2   3   4   5

Keep sober in spirit: 1   2   3   4   5

Fix your hope on the grace of God: 1   2   3   4   5

Put off old habits and behavior: 1   2   3   4   5

Submit to the Holy Spirit: 1   2   3   4   5

☞ Choose your weakest area and make a list below of what you will do this week to strengthen it.

☞ Today and Tomorrow ☜

TODAY: MY JOB IN TIMES OF TRIAL IS TO WORK WITH THE HOLY SPIRIT AT BECOMING MORE LIKE CHRIST.

TOMORROW: I WILL REVIEW THE FIVE AREAS OF PREPAREDNESS AND WORK TO STRENGTHEN MY WEAKEST ONE.

LESSON 6

The Believer's Conduct in a Crisis

 In This Lesson

LEARNING: HOW CAN I OVERCOME THE FEAR THAT OFTEN OVERCOMES ME?

GROWING: WHAT DOES IT MEAN TO FEAR THE LORD?

Once a crisis engulfs us, how are we to behave? Peter makes this general but very powerful statement to the early church as it faced a time of persecution: "Conduct yourselves throughout the time of your stay here in fear" (1 Pet. 1:17). Peter was not referring to being frightened of circumstances or evil people. The fear to which he was referring was a holy awe of the Lord. We are to conduct ourselves with fear of the Lord—reverence, awe, and submission to His majesty. We are to be more in awe of God and His power than we are in awe of man's power or nature's power.

How does a fear of the Lord differ from other types of fear?

How do you react when you are gripped with fear or anxiety? How do you react when you are overcome with fear of the Lord?

A Holy Awe of God's Power to Judge

Those who truly fear God must always remember that God can and will punish the wicked and bring about His purposes and righteousness. We are to stand in awe of the fact that the Lord is a God of absolutes and a God of perfect judgment.

There is a divine balance between God's mercy and judgment. On the one hand, God is merciful, loving, and forgiving to those who turn to Him and receive His forgiveness. He is long-suffering in His patience, allowing men numerous opportunities to turn to Him, confess their sins, and believe in Jesus Christ as their Savior.

But on the other hand, God also judges in righteousness according to the absolutes of His Word. God moves decisively against those who are rebellious toward Him and against those who injure His people. God never winks at sin. All sin is subject to the consequences of suffering, sorrow, and death (Rom. 6:23).

Far more than we fear what man might do, we must fear what God can and will do regarding sin.

And do not fear those who kill the body but cannot kill the soul. But rather fear Him who is able to destroy both soul and body in hell.

—Matthew 10:28

❧ When is fear of danger a healthy response? When is it unhealthy? What distinguishes healthy fear from unhealthy fear?

❧ What does it mean to fear God? How does such a fear influence your life? How does it lead a person to salvation and eternal life?

What Does It Mean to Live in the Fear of the Lord?

There are several practical manifestations of a life lived in fear or awe of the Lord, and these will be the focus of our study.

1. Obedience to God's commandments. The Lord has given us very specific commandments in His Word, and He expects us to keep them—regardless of circumstances. No matter what others may say to us, offering us an alluring, positive, alternative plan to God's commandments, we must never choose to follow their advice. It is a plan that is of man's design, not God's. God's Word is very clear. The problem that most Christians have is not that they do not understand God's standards for right and wrong, but that they choose not to obey what God has said.

A crisis is never a justification for sin. No crisis should ever be used as an excuse to overlook or disobey God's commandments.

If you love Me, keep My commandments.

—John 14:15

Why are love of God and obedience to His commandments inseparable?

↬ Is there an area of disobedience in your life at present? What will you do this week to love God through obedience to His Word?

2. A desire to be like Jesus. Those who love Jesus as their Savior and Lord want to be like Him. Jesus lived in complete obedience to His Father. He did only what the Father told Him to do; He spoke only what the Father prompted Him to say. What Jesus did, we are to do—not to the best of our ability, but to the best of the Holy Spirit's ability within us! The Holy Spirit empowers us to live as Jesus lived. It is our responsibility to ask Him to guide us, help us, counsel us, and to give us the ability to obey. The more we allow the Holy Spirit to work in us and through us, the more we are enabled to be like Jesus and to do what He did.

Jesus knew what it meant to face a crisis. If there was ever a crisis in a person's life, it was the Cross in the life of Jesus! Jesus knew how to face that crisis: in complete submission to the Father's will. Jesus knew both what to say and what to do in the final hours of His earthly life.

When you are in a crisis, ask yourself, "What would Jesus say and do?" Ask the Holy Spirit to show you how Jesus would respond and to help you respond in the same way.

Beloved, now we are children of God; and it has not yet been revealed what we shall be, but we know that when He is revealed, we shall be like Him, for we shall see Him as He is. And everyone who has this hope in Him purifies himself, just as He is pure.

—1 John 3:2, 3

❧ When have you seen a child imitating his parents? How did you imitate your parents when you were young?

❧ As a child of God, how should you be imitating Jesus? How might you imitate Him more fully this week?

3. Courage. Those who fear mankind and fear natural disaster experience a panic that paralyzes. Those who fear the Lord with a holy awe experience a courage that mobilizes them to act! Throughout the Scriptures, we find God's challenge to His people to live in confidence and to respond courageously to life.

Joseph of Arimathea. Joseph of Arimathea found himself in something of a crisis. Jesus had been crucified and His disciples had scattered and gone into hiding. But "Joseph of Arimathea, a prominent council member, who was himself waiting for the kingdom of God, coming and taking courage, went in to Pilate and asked for the body of Jesus" (Mark 15:43).

Peter and John. When the priests, temple leaders, and Sadducees "saw the boldness of Peter and John, and perceived that they were uneducated and untrained men, they marveled. And they realized that they had been with Jesus" (Acts 4:13). Peter and John were not intimidated by this encounter with the religious authorities in Jerusalem. They immediately returned to the believers and reported what had happened. And the believers prayed for them, "Now, Lord, look on their threats, and grant to Your servants that with all boldness they may speak Your word, by stretching out Your hand to heal, and that signs and wonders may be done through the name of Your holy Servant Jesus" (Acts 4:29, 30).

Paul. After Paul had encountered Jesus on the road to Damascus, he "preached boldly at Damascus in the name of Jesus" even though many there distrusted him and counted him as an enemy (see Acts 9:27).

Paul and Barnabas. Envious Jews contradicted and opposed Paul's ministry in Antioch, yet we read that "Paul and Barnabas grew bold and said, 'It was necessary that the word of God should be spoken to you first; but since you reject it, and judge yourselves unworthy of everlasting life, behold, we turn to the Gentiles'" (Acts 13:46).

Rather than cower in the face of crisis or conflict, the early believers became bold. They experienced a manifestation of courage in their lives that was the work of the Holy Spirit in them. When you are in crisis, ask the Lord to give you boldness and courage to speak and do what the Lord prompts you to.

> For you did not receive the spirit of bondage again to fear, but you received the Spirit of adoption by whom we cry out, "Abba, Father."
>
> —Romans 8:15

What does it mean to be in bondage to fear? When have you or someone you know experienced such a state? How did it affect other areas of life?

Abba means "daddy." How can crying out to God as your Father break the bondage of fear?

Our Threefold Response in a Crisis

In summary, Paul advises a threefold response in a time of crisis:

1. Keep God's commandments.
2. Ask the Holy Spirit to help you do what Jesus would do.
3. Have courage! Be bold in your witness to Christ and in presenting the truth of God.

This should be our response to all of life, but especially in crises it is important for us to renew our obedience, our commitment to Christ, and our reliance upon the Holy Spirit. Crises come into every person's life. They tend to arise unexpectedly and quickly. The more we make obedience to God's commandments a way of life, the more we rely upon the Holy Spirit, and the more we display courage in standing up for what is right, the more we will be ready for crises when they come.

> Have I not commanded you? Be strong and of good courage; do not be afraid, nor be dismayed, for the LORD your God is with you wherever you go.
>
> —Joshua 1:9

☙ Why does God command us not to be afraid? What role does one's choice play in dealing with fear? What role do emotions play?

 What is courage? How can one choose to be courageous, regardless of one's emotions?

Today and Tomorrow

TODAY: I CAN BE STRONG AND COURAGEOUS THROUGH THE POWER OF THE HOLY SPIRIT.

TOMORROW: I WILL CONSCIOUSLY IMITATE JESUS THIS WEEK IN WHATEVER SITUATIONS COME MY WAY.

LESSON 7

Living as a Victor

LEARNING: WHY SHOULD I BE THANKFUL WHEN I'M HURTING?

GROWING: WHERE CAN I FIND CONTENTMENT?

What would you most like to change about your circumstances today? Most people would like to change something in their lives: perhaps their job, a family situation, or the state of their health. Some would like to see changes in their finances, others might like to move to a new city. In a great percentage of the cases, the changes are ones that the person believes will make him happier, more at peace, or more secure.

The Bible challenges us not to seek happiness, peace, and security through external changes in our lives, but rather through internal ones. A Christian is empowered to live above circumstances, not under the circumstances, as we commonly say. The apostle Paul was living under house arrest in Rome when he wrote to the Philippians:

> "I have learned in whatever state I am, to be content: I know how to be abased, and I know how to abound . . . I can do all things through Christ who strengthens me."

> —Philippians 4:11–13

76

These verses are about contentment not *with* but *in* a negative situation. Paul's contentment was not a mere feeling or a state of mind, however. It was an attitude that permeated his behavior. His ability to display contentment to others was a powerful witness to his unsaved guards. Consider the results of Paul's deliberate choice to be content within negative circumstances:

> But I want you to know, brethren, that the things which happened to me have actually turned out for the furtherance of the gospel, so that it has become evident to the whole palace guard, and to all the rest, that my chains are in Christ; and most of the brethren in the Lord, having become confident by my chains, are much more bold to speak the word without fear. . . . Christ is preached; and in this I rejoice, yes, and will rejoice.

> —Philippians 1:12–14, 18

What was the source of Paul's contentment, even though he was in prison?

Preach the gospel in prison

What were the results of his contentment? Who was affected by his attitude?

Having become confident by my chains

Paul

The Nature of Contentment

There are two main things that contentment is *not*:

1. Contentment is not denial. Paul was never in denial about his circumstances. He knew that he was imprisoned by Rome. He never tried to hide that fact or to deny that he experienced needs. Paul wrote to the Philippians, "Everywhere and in all things I have learned both to be full and to be hungry, both to abound and to suffer need" (Phil. 4:12). Paul knew the full spectrum of life—the very best of situations, and the very worst of situations.

Read what Paul wrote to Timothy. These are hardly the words of a man who is living in denial of the current gravity of his situation:

> At my first defense no one stood with me, but all forsook me. May it not be charged against them. But the Lord stood with me and strengthened me, so that the message might be preached fully through me, and that all the Gentiles might hear. Also I was delivered out of the mouth of the lion. And the Lord will deliver me from every evil work and preserve me for His heavenly kingdom. To Him be glory forever and ever. Amen!
>
> —2 Timothy 4:16–18

🙠 Why does Paul pray that the sin of abandonment might "not be charged against" those who abandoned him? How might this attitude have contributed to his contentment?

78

≈ Where does Paul find his source of strength and encouragement? How is this attitude different from denying that he is suffering?

2. Contentment is not approval of external conditions. To accept one's external conditions as a current fact is not the same as approving of those conditions. Did Paul want to be free? Absolutely! Did Paul believe that he had been unjustly imprisoned? Did he defend himself vigorously? Did he seek freedom through just and legal means? Most definitely he did!

To be content in a situation is not to say that the condition is good, or even acceptable. It is to say that the state of one's soul within that situation is good and acceptable. It is to say, "My external situation may be negative; I will work diligently to change it. But my internal situation is very positive; I will be steadfast in my relationship with the Lord."

Contentment is not settling down for a settled life. It is not throwing up one's hands and saying, "I give up." It is not throwing in the towel and refusing to work for positive changes. Contentment is not giving in to difficult situations or allowing a negative circumstance to dictate our response to life.

On the contrary, contentment is:

∾ Dwelling peaceably in a current situation until that situation changes. We are to pray, believe, and look for change, but true contentment is trusting God to reveal both His methods and His timing for change.

∾ Refusing to fall into the traps of greed, covetousness, or envy. We are to be content with the possessions that we currently have, without coveting our neighbor's possessions, being envious of another's position, or seeking to hoard or consume far more than we need.

∾ A pervasive attitude of rest that our relationship is right with the Lord. It is an attitude of confidence that God is working all things together for the perfection of His purposes. It is a perspective, a frame of mind, far more than it is a feeling.

Let your conduct be without covetousness; be content with such things as you have. For He Himself has said, "*I will never leave you nor forsake you.*" So we may boldly say: "*The Lord is my helper; I will not fear. What can man do to me?*"

—Hebrews 13:5–6

∾ Why does the author of Hebrews equate covetousness with fear in these verses? How can covetousness lead to fear and anxiety?

☙ Why are we commanded to *be* content, rather than to pray that we'll *find* contentment? What role does our will play in the process?

How Can We Develop Inner Contentment?

The Bible gives us three things that we can do to develop inner contentment so that we live as victors even when we seem to be losing the battle.

1. Focus on the positive circumstances around you. No situation is one hundred-percent negative. There is always a positive side to every experience, every situation. Look for it. There are some good things around you even in the worst of times.

Refuse to wallow in a pity party. Refuse to complain, criticize, or justify a negative situation. Constant conversation or comments about a negative situation only make that situation loom larger in your own mind, as well as in the thinking of others around you.

Again, this focus on the positive is not a denial that negative things exist. Rather, it is a choice to put one's focus and attention on the positive things that can be built up, improved, encouraged, or praised. When we focus on the positive, even as we work to change the negative, we live in victory over the enemy. We are in a much better position to bring about the true change that results in positive growth and lasting reconciliation.

> Finally, brethren, whatever things are true, whatever things are noble, whatever things are just, whatever things are pure, whatever things are lovely, whatever things are of good report, if there is any virtue and if there is anything praiseworthy— meditate on these things.
>
> —Philippians 4:8

❧ Define the following in your own words, giving real-life examples of each:

True:

Noble:

Just:

Pure:

Lovely:

Good report:

Virtue:

Praiseworthy:

2. Witness to someone about the love of God and the saving grace of Jesus Christ. Some people think that, if they are going through a negative experience, others will not view them as being victorious spiritually and, therefore, will not receive a positive witness about Christ. Some fear that others will equate a negative circumstance with a lack of faith or punishment from God. The real problem is that people who are going through hard times often think these things about themselves!

No matter what you are experiencing, no matter how grave the situation, you can always give a positive witness about Christ's sustaining grace, His forgiveness, His mercy, His love, and His authority over all evil. In pointing to Christ, you point to the source of solution to every problem—not only your problem. Choose to be a positive witness to Christ's saving, healing, and restoring power.

But you be watchful in all things, endure afflictions, do the work of an evangelist, fulfill your ministry.

—2 Timothy 4:5

What does it mean to be "watchful in all things"? How is this accomplished? How does it strengthen contentment?

What is the work of an evangelist? How does fulfilling one's ministry help a person to gain contentment?

3. Choose to act in a positive manner, seeking positive results. Don't act out of your pain; respond in faith that God can do something good in the midst of dark or troubling times. When Paul was thrown into prison in Rome, he founded a church! He closed his letter to the Philippians this way: "The brethren who are with me greet you. All the saints greet you, but especially those who are of Caesar's household" (Phil. 4:21, 22).

Members of the praetorian guard of Caesar, the emperor's personal guards, were being won to Christ through Paul's imprisonment. Paul was not only evangelizing the men who were guarding him, but he also was teaching and strengthening these new converts, helping to establish a new branch to the church in Rome.

Refuse to make decisions or take actions that will make matters worse. Watch closely what you say to others, especially those who have hurt you or who are responsible for your negative situation. Those who find themselves in a negative marital situation often begin to speak about separation or divorce. They hurl abusive and critical comments at their spouse. Very often, those who find themselves feeling guilty or hurt begin to lash out with accusations or threats. Actions such as these only intensify a negative situation—they do very little to bring healing and reconciliation.

But I say to you who hear: Love your enemies, do good to those who hate you, bless those who curse you, and pray for those who spitefully use you. To him who strikes you on the one cheek, offer the other also. And from him who takes away your cloak, do not withhold your tunic either.

—Luke 6:27–29

☙ When have you retaliated in anger against someone who offended you? What was the result of that response?

☙ What does it mean, in practical terms, to offer the other cheek when someone smites you? To offer your tunic to someone who takes your cloak?

Living as a Victor

Stop to think a moment about a person who exhibits these traits:

- ❧ Deep inner contentment based upon a right relationship with God
- ❧ Realistic about life, but working to change those things that are negative
- ❧ Focused on the positive
- ❧ Quick to give a word of witness about Jesus Christ
- ❧ Engaged in positive behaviors toward others, seeking positive results

You would probably describe such a person as being victorious in his Christian walk! We are called to live victoriously because we are in association with the Victor of all life, Jesus Christ. Others who see us in the midst of trouble and trials should find their attention drawn toward Christ in us, rather than toward the problems that surround us. We should proclaim with our lives as well as our words, "Thanks be to God, who gives us the victory through our Lord Jesus Christ" (1 Cor. 15:57).

Now godliness with contentment is great gain. For we brought nothing into this world, and it is certain we can carry nothing out. And having food and clothing, with these we shall be content.

—1 Timothy 6:6–8

Why does Paul say that contentment *with* godliness is great gain? What would result from contentment without godliness? Godliness without contentment?

Paul lists food and clothing as sufficient for contentment. What has he *not* listed as requirements? What things do you put on the list of "must have before I'm content"?

Today and Tomorrow

TODAY: CONTENTMENT IS A CHOICE, NOT AN EXTERNAL CONDITION.

TOMORROW: I WILL CONSCIOUSLY WORK ON BEING CONTENT IN THE COMING WEEK.

LESSON 8

Confronting Four Giant Fears

─────── ❧ In This Lesson ☙ ───────

LEARNING: WHAT HAPPENS IF MY GREATEST FEARS COME TRUE?

GROWING: HOW CAN I FIND SECURITY WHEN THREATENED WITH DEATH OR
POVERTY?

─────── ⌘ ───────

"Fear not" is one of the foremost commands in the Bible. The Lord makes it very clear in His Word that He wants His people to live in intimate relationship with Him forever—a relationship without fear of punishment—and in this world, to live as overcomers of fear. The Lord never chides people for feeling fear—it is a normal human response to pain, trouble, and trauma. But the Lord does call us to overcome fear with our faith.

We discussed fear briefly in an earlier lesson, but in this lesson I want to focus on the four great fears that all people face to some degree during their lifetimes. These fears can loom to giant-sized proportions in times of trial or crisis. The Bible addresses each of these four fears in a direct way and with many verses. We will only be able to deal with a few of the many references. If you struggle with fear in one of these areas, I encourage you to use a concordance and make a personal study of God's Word on the subject, including God's promises to help you overcome fear.

1. The Fear of Death

Psychologists tell us that the number one fear of all people is the fear of death. This certainly is understandable, since death brings both finality and judgment. Once we die, we can no longer relive those moments that we wish we could have lived a different way. Things that we have done or left undone will be our legacy and reputation in the generations ahead. (See Jesus' parable in Luke 16:19–31.)

The Bible speaks of death as an appointment that we all must keep: "It is appointed for men to die once" (Heb. 9:27). The Bible also speaks of judgment in relationship to death. This same verse in Hebrews continues, ". . . but after this the judgment." The Bible also holds out hope for the believer regarding judgment. Hebrews 9:28 concludes, "So Christ was offered once to bear the sins of many. To those who eagerly wait for Him He will appear a second time, apart from sin, for salvation."

> And as it is appointed for men to die once, but after this the judgment, so Christ was offered once to bear the sins of many. To those who eagerly wait for Him He will appear a second time, apart from sin, for salvation.
>
> —Hebrews 9:27, 28

What does it mean that "it is appointed for men to die once"? Why is this a universal truth, that all men must die? Where did death come from?

⚞ What judgment is the author of Hebrews referring to? How does Christ's death set Christians free from that judgment?

Those who die in Christ are instantly with the Lord. They will see Him face to face, and live in a paradise that is free from sin. As Jesus said to the thief on the cross who believed in Him: "Assuredly, I say to you, today you will be with Me in Paradise" (Luke 23:43). As believers in Christ, we are saved from the consequences of our sin and given eternal life, and we are going to be saved from this sinful world—we are going to live in an eternal home that is totally sin-free.

Paul described death as a change—one moment here, the next changed and with Christ forever. We will be free from our earthly bodies, which are prone to sickness, decay, and corruption. We will live in incorruptible bodies that are glorious, powerful, and immortal. What a wonderful life lies just beyond death for the believer! In times of trouble and trauma, hold on to that hope. Put your trust in the Lord to be the first One you see as you enter into eternity.

So also is the resurrection of the dead. The body is sown in corruption, it is raised in incorruption. It is sown in dishonor, it is raised in glory. It is sown in weakness, it is raised in power. It is sown a natural body, it is raised a spiritual body. There is a natural body, and there is a spiritual body.

—1 Corinthians 15:42–44

What are the differences between the natural body and the spiritual body? According to these verses, what must happen before one can attain the spiritual body?

What dishonor is Paul referring to in connection with the natural body? What corruption is he referring to? What will it be like to have a body that is free from these things?

2. The Fear of Failure and Rejection

A major fear that people experience in times of trouble is a fear of failure. Sickness, loss of a job, an accident—all of these can be reasons for a person to feel as if he has failed in some way.

The main reason that we fear failure is that others might reject us or view us with disdain if we fail. We all want to be liked and to be in warm association with other people. We want to be appreciated, applauded, valued, and considered worthy. When we fail, we fear the loss of friendships, work relationships, family associations, and even loss of relationships with people in the church.

When we speak of failure, of course, we are not referring to sinful behavior but to those times when we attempt to do right but fall short in some way. Yet even when we do sin, the Lord does not reject us. Our Father regards our failures as potential learning experiences for us, an opportunity to mold our character into greater conformity to Christ, and an opportunity for His own strength and power to be manifested.

The apostle Paul experienced a "thorn in his flesh" that others perceived as a sign of weakness or failure. Paul wrote, "Concerning this thing I pleaded with the Lord three times that it might depart from me. And He said to me, 'My grace is sufficient for you, for My strength is made perfect in weakness'" (2 Cor. 12:8). Paul concluded about this failure:

> And He said to me, "My grace is sufficient for you, for My strength is made perfect in weakness." Therefore most gladly I will rather boast in my infirmities, that the power of Christ may rest upon me. Therefore I take pleasure in infirmities, in reproaches, in needs, in persecutions, in distresses, for Christ's sake. For when I am weak, then I am strong.
>
> —2 Corinthians 12:9, 10

∾ In what ways is God's strength "made perfect in weakness"? Give practical examples.

∾ What pleasure did Paul find when he suffered infirmities, reproaches, persecutions, distress, and so forth? What pleasure can you take during times of hardship?

We can also know with certainty from God's Word that no failure on our part will cause the Lord to leave us. Moses said to Joshua in the sight of all the Israelites:

> "Be strong and of good courage, for you must go with this people to the land which the LORD has sworn to their fathers to give them, and you shall cause them to inherit it. And the LORD, He is the One who goes before you. He will be with you, He will not leave you nor forsake you; do not fear nor be dismayed."
>
> —Deuteronomy 31:7, 8

Nothing that we do can cause the lord to turn His back on us or disown His association with us. He is forever present with us, now and every moment of our future, on into eternity.

When we fail, the Lord requires only that we turn to Him and ask His forgiveness, His wisdom, and His help. We must be quick to obey the Lord if He shows us areas in which we must seek forgiveness of others or make amends for our errors. Our humility before the Lord permits Him to heal us, restore us, and bring us into close fellowship with other believers.

This does not mean that all broken relationships will be reconciled on earth. The will and humility of both persons in a broken relationship must be involved for a relationship to be reconciled by God. It does mean, however, that the Lord desires to heal all broken hearts.

> A father of the fatherless, a defender of widows, is God in His holy habitation. God sets the solitary in families; He brings out those who are bound into prosperity; but the rebellious dwell in a dry land.
>
> —Psalm 68:5, 6

ᑭ How do the qualities of God listed in these verses relate to a fear of rejection?

ᑭ What does it mean to "dwell in a dry land"? How is this the opposite of experiencing God's loving care?

3. The Fear of Material Loss

Times of tragedy, and especially tragedies that involve natural or economic disasters, are often accompanied by a great fear of material loss. We fear that we will lose our possessions that have given us a degree of comfort, status, and security. For some, the loss may be severe to the point of fearing homelessness or poverty.

We need to remember always that all things which we count as possessions have been given to us by the Lord. He is the One who gives us the ability to work, to create, to produce, and to acquire wealth. He is the One who presents opportunities to us and allows our efforts to prosper. As Ecclesiastes 5:19 tells us, "As for every man to whom God has given riches and wealth, and given him power to eat of it, to receive his heritage and rejoice in his labor—this is the gift of God." The Lord asks us to trust Him to provide what we need, and admonishes us against putting our trust in possessions or money.

Furthermore, whatever we may lose in terms of material possessions, the Lord is able to restore. In times of loss, we must trust God to teach us the lessons that He wants us to learn and to restore to us anything that the enemy of our souls has stolen from us or destroyed.

> Which of you by worrying can add one cubit to his stature? So why do you worry about clothing? Consider the lilies of the field, how they grow: they neither toil nor spin; and yet I say to you that even Solomon in all his glory was not arrayed like one of these. Now if God so clothes the grass of the field, which today is, and tomorrow is thrown into the oven, will He not much more clothe you, O you of little faith?
>
> —Matthew 6:27–30

Why does Jesus refer to His audience as "you of little faith"? What part does faith play in resisting fear and worry?

✍ Why does Jesus refer to grass and flowers to address basic human needs? What point is He trying to make?

4. The Fear of Change

In times of trauma and hardship, many people feel as if their entire world is shaken and nothing will ever be the same again. They fear the unknown elements of the future. They do not trust God to deal kindly with them in the days ahead. In their thinking, all change is bad change. The fact is, a great deal of change is for our good!

Jeremiah spoke the words of the Lord to Judah in a time of great upheaval and turmoil. The people longed to hear words of comfort from the prophet—they deeply desired a message that the Lord was going to deliver them from being taken captive by Babylon. The Lord, however, told them that they would be taken captive for seventy years!

But the word of the Lord to His people did not end with that message. The Lord also told His people, "The days are coming . . . that I will bring back from captivity My people Israel and Judah . . . And I will cause them to return to the land that I gave their fathers, and they shall possess it" (Jer. 30:3). Furthermore, the Lord said:

"Therefore do not fear, O My servant Jacob," says the Lord, "Nor be dismayed, O Israel; for behold, I will save you from afar, and your seed from the land of their captivity. Jacob shall return, have rest and be quiet, and no one shall make him afraid. For I am with you," says the Lord, "to save you; though I make a full end of all nations where I have scattered you, yet I will not make a complete end of you. But I will correct you in justice, and will not let you go altogether unpunished."

—Jeremiah 30:10–11

The Lord used the years of captivity to teach very important lessons to His people—lessons that prepared them for the return of their land and future prosperity.

Furthermore, the Lord said to His people:

For I know the thoughts that I think toward you, says the Lord, thoughts of peace and not of evil, to give you a future and a hope.

—Jeremiah 29:11

Any time we are facing change, we must remember that the Lord has the same desire for us that He had for the Israelites; His plans for us lead to peace and not evil. He has a good future for us, and, therefore, we must have hope! Choose to see change as a process of good that the Lord is unfolding in your life. Trust Him to lead you to greater prosperity and wholeness.

❧ The Lord had told the people of Judah that He was about to send them into captivity in Babylon as a result of their idolatry. Why, then, did He command them not to be afraid?

❧ What does it mean that the Lord would correct Judah in justice (Jer. 30:11)? How does God's justice bring blessings out of punishment?

Saying No to Fear

Faith is saying no to fear and yes to God. Our faith that we will be with the Lord beyond our death gives us the courage to say no to a fear of death. Our faith that God will never forsake us, regardless of how we may fail, gives us the courage to say no to the fear of failure and rejection. Our faith that God desires to prosper us and meet our needs gives us the courage to say no to a fear of material loss. Our faith that God is leading us through life, step by step, gives us the courage to say no to a fear of change.

Our faith is rooted in who God is and what He will do. Choose to walk by faith and respond to life with faith, rather than cowering before trouble. Let us remember the words of Paul to the Corinthians: For we walk by faith, not by sight (2 Cor. 5:7).

> The LORD is my shepherd; I shall not want. He makes me to lie down in green pastures; He leads me beside the still waters. He restores my soul; He leads me in the paths of righteousness for His name's sake.
>
> —Psalm 23:1–3

☙ Put each of the metaphors from these verses ("lie down in green pastures," etc.) into your own words, and give examples of each from your own life.

What does David mean when he says that God does these things "for His name's sake"? How is God's name involved in the circumstances of our lives?

Today and Tomorrow

TODAY: ABSOLUTELY NOTHING CAN HAPPEN TO ME WITHOUT GOD'S APPROVAL.

TOMORROW: I WILL CONSCIOUSLY SAY NO TO FEAR THIS WEEK, REMEMBERING THAT GOD IS IN CONTROL.

LESSON 9

A Focus on Our Destiny as Believers

---------------- ❧ **In This Lesson** ❧ ----------------

LEARNING: WHAT IS THE PURPOSE OF LIFE, ANYWAY?

GROWING: HOW CAN I KNOW IF I'M DOING GOD'S WILL FOR MY LIFE?

❧

All followers of Christ have the destiny of an eternal life with our loving heavenly Father. That is our ultimate destiny. But what is your destiny here on earth? What purposes does God have for believers during their earthly lives?

To a degree, our purpose on earth is highly personalized. We are unique creatures, gifted and talented in unique ways, and called to unique ministries within a unique sphere of influence. We each face the challenge of discovering precisely what the Lord created us to be and to do.

In a more general way, however, all of us are given a purpose as followers of Christ. In this lesson, we are going to focus on five of these general purposes related to our destiny as believers.

1. Our Destiny Is to Show God's Love to the World

Part of our purpose as believers is to express God's love to a love-starved world. Every Christian should believe that God loves him and should display his belief to others. God's love is infinite and unconditional. It is far greater, far richer, and far more meaningful than any of us can fully grasp. Nevertheless, we are to grow in our ability to accept God's love and in our ability to express God's love to others. That is part of our destiny and purpose on earth.

God's love does not change. God's love does not waver, wax, or wane. It is constant. As James says, "There is no variation or shadow of turning" with God's love (James 1:17). Love is part of his unchanging nature (1 John 4:8)

God's love is unconditional. God loves you as much as He will ever love you, even though you are far from perfect. Romans 5:8 tells us plainly, "God demonstrates His own love toward us, in that while we were still sinners, Christ died for us." Nothing that you or anyone else can do can separate you from God's love. And nothing that you do can ever cause God to love you more. He already loves you with an infinite love.

God's love motivates Him toward our blessing and perfection. God loves us as we are, but because He loves us, He does not leave us as we are. God's desire is that we draw closer and closer to Him. As He conforms us more and more into the character and likeness of Jesus Christ, we become more and more whole, and we grow into greater and greater intimacy and fellowship with Him.

Our response to God's love. Our response to God's love is very clear: We are commanded to love others. Our purpose and destiny on earth is to receive God's love and to display His love to others. The world needs to experience God's love, especially in troubled times. It is in the darkest hours that love shines the brightest.

We love Him because He first loved us. If someone says, "I love God," and hates his brother, he is a liar; for he who does not love his brother whom he has seen, how can he love God whom he has not seen? And this commandment we have from Him: that he who loves God must love his brother also.

—1 John 4:19–21

➢ Why is it impossible to love God without also loving other Christians? How does this principle apply to loving non-Christians? (See Luke 10.)

➢ According to these verses from 1 John, where does our love for God originate?

2. Our Destiny Is to Proclaim Jesus as the Savior

Part of your purpose on earth is to receive Jesus Christ as your Savior, and then to proclaim Him as the Savior to others through your words and deeds. Paul stated this message of salvation:

He has delivered us from the power of darkness and conveyed us into the kingdom of the Son of His love, in whom we have redemption through His blood, the forgiveness of sins. . . . For it pleased the Father that in Him all the fullness should dwell, and by Him to reconcile all things to Himself, by Him, whether things on earth or things in heaven, having made peace through the blood of His cross. And you, who once were alienated and enemies in your mind by wicked works, yet now He has reconciled in the body of His flesh through death, to present you holy, and blameless, and above reproach in His sight.

—Colossians 1:13–14, 19–22

🕯 Put Paul's message of salvation into your own words. How would you explain these truths to an unbelieving friend?

We are to proclaim to others that:

🕯 they do not need to live with a sin nature, steeped in guilt and shame before Christ.

🕯 Jesus Christ died as God's atoning sacrifice for sin so that they do not need to reap the consequences of their sin, which is eternal separation from God.

🕯 we can experience salvation by believing in Jesus Christ as God's atoning sacrifice and accepting what He did on the Cross on our behalf.

᭠ when we receive Jesus Christ as our Savior, Christ sends the Holy Spirit to indwell us so that we might live blameless and holy before God.

Jesus Christ did not only come to save us from sin, but to save us from sin's hold on our lives. We can live in freedom from the bondage of a nature that desires to sin. We can live as unto the Lord. What good news this is! We are to be ambassadors—witnesses, messengers—of this good news to all whom we encounter. When times are unsettled or difficult, the world is far more ready to hear this message of Jesus Christ as Savior. We must be quick to speak of the saving love of God to others who are experiencing trouble or who may be facing death.

Now then, we are ambassadors for Christ, as though God were pleading through us: we implore you on Christ's behalf, be reconciled to God.

—2 Corinthians 5:20

᭠ In what sense is God pleading with the unsaved through you? How does He use your life and words to reach others?

᭠ What implication does this have on your life's goals?

3. Our Destiny Is to Live a Godly Life

Our destiny as believers is to live a godly life and to keep God's commandments to the very best of our ability. Our purpose is to show others, through our behavior and conversations, that it is possible to live a pure, peaceful, joyful life on earth. Our purpose is to reflect a life that is totally reliant upon the Holy Spirit for guidance into right decisions, right choices, and right actions.

When times of trouble arise, those in the world look for examples of goodness. They look for those who are living in purity and who have faith and confidence. They look for examples that say to them, "Yes, it is possible even in the midst of terrible circumstances, to serve God." You are called by God to be such an example. Your destiny and purpose on earth are to live a righteous life according to all that the Lord commands you.

> For you are the temple of the living God. As God has said: *"I will dwell in them and walk among them. I will be their God, and they shall be My people."* Therefore *"Come out from among them and be separate, says the Lord. Do not touch what is unclean, and I will receive you."*

> —2 Corinthians 6:16–17

What does it mean to be the temple of God? What implications does this have on your life? On your destiny?

What does it mean to "come out from among" unbelievers? How is this balanced with the Lord's command to take the gospel to the unsaved?

4. Our Destiny Is to Serve Others

We each have been given both natural gifts and ministry gifts in order that we might serve others. Part of our purpose on earth is to be involved in active ministry to others—which means meeting needs in their lives. To the best of our ability, we are to meet the practical and material needs of others, as well as their emotional, physical, and spiritual needs. We are to pray for others, serve others, give to others, and be available to others. Times of trouble and trauma are times of great need. Our purpose on earth is to meet needs in the name of Jesus.

Be kindly affectionate to one another with brotherly love, in honor giving preference to one another; not lagging in diligence, fervent in spirit, serving the Lord; rejoicing in hope, patient in tribulation, continuing steadfastly in prayer; distributing to the needs of the saints, given to hospitality.

—Romans 12:10–13

109

﹌ Make a list below of the things that Paul commands us to do in these verses, putting each into your own words.

﹌ What attitude does Paul command us to have when serving others?

5. Our Destiny Is to Praise God in All Situations

Part of our destiny and purpose on earth is to praise God. Jesus said that, if we don't praise God, the stones will cry out in praise (Luke 19:37–40). God delights in our praise. He responds to our praise. He uses our praise to defeat our enemies.

In times of struggle and difficulty, it is especially important that we fulfill our destiny to praise God. The world watches and listens. Will we curse God in times of trouble, as Job's wife encouraged him to do, or will we praise God for who He is and what we believe He will do on our behalf? May we always choose to lift our voices in praise!

A Source of Encouragement

What type of person do you want to have with you in a time of trouble? Isn't it someone who is loving toward you and reminds you of God's love, who reminds you that Jesus Christ is your Savior and that you are forever secure in God's forgiveness, who lives a godly life, who is quick to see your needs and meet them, who voices praise to God? We are called by God to be just that type of person to others. Our destiny and purpose on the earth are to be Christ-followers—to love others, serve others, praise God, and live godly lives!

> Bless the LORD, O my soul, and forget not all His benefits: Who forgives all your iniquities, who heals all your diseases, who redeems your life from destruction, who crowns you with lovingkindness and tender mercies, who satisfies your mouth with good things, so that your youth is renewed like the eagle's.
>
> —Psalm 103:2–5

List below the qualities of God's character listed in these verses, putting them in your own words and giving examples from your own life. Add others to the list as the Lord brings them to mind, then return to this list every day this week and spend time praising God.

Today and Tomorrow

TODAY: THE LORD'S PURPOSE FOR MY LIFE IS TO PRAISE HIM AND SERVE OTHERS.

TOMORROW: I WILL SPEND TIME PRAISING GOD EACH DAY THIS WEEK, AND ASK HIM TO SHOW ME OPPORTUNITIES TO SERVE OTHERS.

Five Prayers that God Answers in Rough Times

☙ In This Lesson ☚

LEARNING: DOES GOD REALLY ANSWER PRAYER?

GROWING: HOW SHOULD I PRAY DURING THIS TIME OF HARDSHIP?

Is it right to pray that God removes our trouble, heals our bodies, reconciles our marriages, or removes our pain? Absolutely! The Bible encourages us to pray diligently in times of trouble, and to do so with faith, trusting God to act for our eternal benefit and according to His perfect methods and timing. In this lesson, we will look at five prayers that we are wise to pray in times of trouble.

1. "Lord, Alleviate This Pressure"

In the Bible, stress and pressure are often described in terms of oppression—a feeling of heaviness, as if the weight of the world is on one's shoulders. Jesus said that He came to fulfill these words of the prophet Isaiah:

The Spirit of the Lord GOD is upon Me,
Because the LORD has anointed Me
To preach good tidings to the poor;
He has sent Me to heal the brokenhearted,
To proclaim liberty to the captives,
And the opening of the prison to those who are bound. . .
To comfort all who mourn,
To console those who mourn in Zion,
To give them beauty for ashes,
The oil of joy for mourning,
The garment of praise for the spirit of heaviness.

—Isaiah 61:1–3

◈ How does the gospel of Jesus Christ meet all the needs mentioned in these verses?

◈ What is a garment of praise? How is it attained? How does praising God actually reduce stress?

When we are feeling oppressed, stressed out, or frustrated because life seems overwhelming, we need to pray that the Lord will rebuke the enemy for our sake and restore our joy. The Lord also desires that we live free of worry and anxiety. Worry is a form of doubt, and it can cause us to feel great pressure. The more we worry, the less we sleep, the more likely we are to make hurried and unwise decisions, and the more prone we are to accidents. Worry increases pressure, rather than reducing it. If worry is the source of your pressure, ask the Lord to help you trust Him more (see Mark 9:24).

2. "Lord, Clarify This Confusion"

The Lord is never the instigator of confusion. His commandments are clear. His path is well lighted. His message is direct. His desire is for order and peace among His people. As Paul wrote to the Ephesians, "Walk worthy of the calling with which you were called . . . endeavoring to keep the unity of the Spirit in the bond of peace" (Eph. 4:1, 3). Paul also admonished the church, "How is it then, brethren? Whenever you come together, each of you has a psalm, has a teaching, has a tongue, has a revelation, has an interpretation. Let all things be done for edification. . . . Let all things be done decently and in order" (1 Cor. 14:26, 40).

Two words are closely related to *confusion* in the Bible: *deceit* and *hypocrisy*. Deceit is a lie—and lies always breed confusion. Hypocrisy is being two-faced—and again, hypocrisy results in confusion. Any time that we are confused, we should look to see if deceit or hypocrisy is the cause of our confusion.

The prayer that we must pray when we feel confused is this: "Lord, shed the light of Your truth on this matter. Deliver me from hypocrisy. Bring order to my thinking. Bring order to this group [or this marriage, or this meeting, or this place, or this experience]."

For where envy and self-seeking exist, confusion and every evil thing are there. But the wisdom that is from above is first pure, then peaceable, gentle, willing to yield, full of mercy and good fruits, without partiality and without hypocrisy.

—James 3:16–17

ᴇᴇ How do envy and selfishness breed confusion? What is necessary for such confusion to be cleared away?

ᴇᴇ How do hypocrisy and favoritism breed confusion? What is necessary for such confusion to be cleared away?

3. "Lord, Help Me with This Pain"

The pain that we experience in rough times is not only physical, but also emotional and spiritual. We ache in sorrow and grief, and as a result of mental anguish.

When you are experiencing pain, ask the Lord to heal you, both in your body and in your emotions.

> Is anyone among you suffering? Let him pray. Is anyone cheerful? Let him sing psalms. Is anyone among you sick? Let him call for the elders of the church, and let them pray over him, anointing him with oil in the name of the Lord. And the prayer of faith will save the sick, and the Lord will raise him up. And if he has committed sins, he will be forgiven.
>
> —James 5:13–15

What part do praise and prayer play in physical healing, according to these verses? How does this compare with the world's views?

In what sense is the entire body of Christ involved in these verses? How does this apply to asking the Lord for healing?

4. "Lord, Help Me Withstand This Temptation"

We must never think that the Lord tempts us to do evil. James wrote very plainly about this:

> Let no one say when he is tempted, "I am tempted by God"; for God cannot be tempted by evil, nor does He Himself tempt anyone. But each one is tempted when he is drawn away by his own desires and enticed. Then, when desire has conceived, it gives birth to sin; and sin, when it is full-grown, brings forth death.
>
> —James 1:13–15

What are the steps leading to death, according to these verses? What is involved in each step along the way?

How does desire conceive? How does it give birth to sin? What does sin become when it is "full-grown"?

The word for *tempt* in the Bible can also mean "test." The Lord does test us from time to time—not for His sake, but so that we will discover areas of weakness, error, or rebellion in our lives. The purpose of the Lord's test is that we might make changes in our lives and move on to greater strength and to a deeper level of intimacy with the Lord. But—and this is very important—the Lord never tests us by tempting us to break His commandments. The devil is the one who is called "the tempter" in the Bible; he comes to entice us to do evil (see Matt. 4:1–4). When we feel a temptation to do evil, we must pray quickly as Jesus taught us, "Deliver us from the evil one" (Matt. 6:13).

Furthermore, the Lord never allows the enemy to tempt us beyond what we are able to bear. He always provides the way of escape for us (1 Cor. 10:13). We are wise to ask the Lord to reveal to us His escape plan!

> No temptation has overtaken you except such as is common to man; but God is faithful, who will not allow you to be tempted beyond what you are able, but with the temptation will also make the way of escape, that you may be able to bear it.
>
> —1 Corinthians 10:13

🔖 Note that Paul speaks of *the* way of escape, rather than *a* way. What is this way of escape from temptation?

◈ Why does the Lord permit us to be tempted by the devil? What does He want to accomplish in our lives?

5. "Lord, Give Me Strength to Endure"

The Lord makes numerous promises in His Word that He will be the "strong right arm" of those who love Him and obey His commandments. He tells us that He is our rock, our fortress, our high tower—all of which are places of refuge that a person might run to when enduring rough times.

The Lord gives us His power so that we might outlast and overcome hard times, He gives us His presence and authority so that we might fight and win spiritual battles, and He gives us His Word so that we might defeat the enemy with it (see Matt. 4:1–11). He sends His holy angels to be ministering servants on our behalf and to defend us in our stand against evil. When you are experiencing a rough time, pray to the Lord for enduring strength! Pray for spiritual power!

> The LORD is my light and my salvation; whom shall I fear? The LORD is the strength of my life; of whom shall I be afraid? For in the time of trouble He shall hide me in His pavilion; in the secret place of His tabernacle He shall hide me; He shall set me high upon a rock.
>
> —Psalm 27:1, 5

⨠ What metaphors of God's protection does David use here? What does each say about God's character?

⨠ What is required of a person if he is to find safety in a pavilion? On a high rock? What does this suggest about your role in finding God's strength?

Expect God to Answer!

When you pray, expect God to both hear and answer your prayers. Trust Him to be faithful to His Word and to deliver you from the anguish of your difficult experience. Trust Him to give you peace in your heart that is beyond understanding.

Make Philippians 4:6–7 your hope as you pray: "In everything by prayer and supplication, with thanksgiving, let your requests be made known to God; and the peace of God, which surpasses all understanding, will guard your hearts and minds through Christ Jesus."

Take Heart and Have Courage!

Of one thing you can be certain in any time of trouble, suffering, pain, or tragedy: The Lord is with you! Time and again in His Word, the Lord assures us of His presence:

The LORD is with you while you are with Him. If you seek Him, He will be found by you; but if you forsake Him, He will forsake you.

—2 Chronicles 15:2

You will not need to fight in this battle. Position yourselves, stand still and see the salvation of the LORD, who is with you. . . . Do not fear or be dismayed.

—2 Chronicles 20:17

"Do not be afraid of him," says the LORD, "for I am with you, to save you and deliver you from his hand."

—Jeremiah 42:11

"Be strong, all you people of the land," says the LORD, "and work; for I am with you," says the LORD of hosts.

—Haggai 2:4

Jesus also said to His disciples, "I am with you always" (Matt. 28:20). Truly, if the Lord is with us, and "if God is for us, who can be against us?" (Rom. 8:31). When rough times come, immerse yourself in God's Word. Read His promises to you, His beloved child. Read about His power, His strength, His wisdom, and His love. Read how He has helped countless men and women through the ages as they trusted in Him. Read about His saving, delivering, and restoring power.

The more you read and study God's Word, the stronger your faith will grow. The more you trust God, the more you will grow in your understanding that He is trustworthy in all things, at all times. The more you take courage in the Lord's presence with you, the more secure you will feel—even in the most troubling times and the most trying circumstances. The Lord is our Security, every moment of our lives.

Be anxious for nothing, but in everything by prayer and supplication, with thanksgiving, let your requests be made known to God; and the peace of God, which surpasses all understanding, will guard your hearts and minds through Christ Jesus.

—Philippians 4:6–7

🔖 Why does Paul include thanksgiving with our prayers of supplication? What part does a thankful spirit play in making requests?

🔖 What does it mean that God's peace will guard our hearts and minds? What role does your mind play in facing trials? What role does your heart play?

🔖 Today and Tomorrow ✒

TODAY: GOD ALWAYS ANSWERS PRAYER.

TOMORROW: I WILL SPEND EXTRA TIME THIS WEEK IN PRAYER, SEEKING GOD'S STRENGTH AND DIRECTION.

9 781418 543754